The Tea Dance

A play for women

Margaret Bower

Samuel French – London
New York – Sydney – Toronto – Hollywood

CHARACTERS

Olive Adams, a pretty middle-aged woman, recently
   divorced
Jean Barbour, her unmarried sister
Barbara Lane, a widow — quite a merry one
Lucy, the maid
The Woman (non-speaking)
Mrs Chisholm (Agatha Christie)
Mary Day, her secretary/companion

The action takes place in a small sitting-room adjacent to
the ballroom in the hotel on Burgh Island

Time — 1936

AUTHOR'S NOTE

Olive, Jean and Barbara are all middle-aged, reasonably attractive and financially secure, but for various reasons are all without male partners, and therefore lead much more restricted lives than they would nowadays. Being on holiday and craving a little excitement, it is not surprising that they let their imaginations run riot when something unexpected does happen.

Burgh Island is a real island off the South Devon coast. The hotel is a real hotel. Agatha Christie was a regular visitor there and local rumour has it that Wallis Simpson was also a visitor once.

M.B.

THE TEA DANCE

A small sitting-room adjacent to the ballroom in the hotel on Burgh Island. Mid-afternoon on a summer's day in 1936

The room is furnished with wicker chairs and tables, potted palms etc. There is a bookcase on one wall and a window in the "fourth" wall overlooking the sea. A pair of binoculars is on the window ledge. There are two doorways, one leading to the ballroom and one to the rest of the hotel

A tea dance is in progress and the sound of music can be heard throughout the action of the play

As the Curtain *rises Mrs Olive Adams and her sister Miss Jean Barbour are sitting at one of the small tables, drinking tea and listening to the music from the ballroom. The music finishes, there is a ripple of applause and after a moment or two Mrs Barbara Lane enters from the ballroom, fanning herself. She sinks into a chair*

Barbara That was lovely. I haven't danced for years.

Olive I find that difficult to believe. You looked quite the expert on the floor. Very professional.

Barbara We danced a lot, my husband and I, but that was a long time ago. I'm quite rusty nowadays.

Olive Well, you certainly didn't look it. We were most impressed, weren't we, Jean?

Barbara That was because I had an excellent partner. It makes all the difference.

Jean Yes, who was that charming gentleman you were dancing with?

Barbara Mr Purdy. Isn't he a sweetie—and so is his wife. She is the rheumaticky lady with the two sticks. Obviously she can't dance, though I gather they were very keen before she was ill. Anyway, she sent her husband over to ask me. Wasn't that kind?

Jean Poor soul. It must be very hard for her.

Olive I'm sure the sea air can't be good for her. The West Country never was the healthiest place for rheumatics. I wonder why they chose to come here.

Barbara I've no idea, but I'll ask them if you like. I shall be going
  back to dance again in a minute. I left Mr Purdy having tea with
  his wife. They did ask me to join them but I thought better not. I
  don't want Mrs Purdy to think I'm making a take-over bid for
  her husband.

Jean Ring the bell and the maid will bring you a tray of tea here.

Barbara No thanks, I really don't want any tea. I'm just on my
  way to my room to freshen up.

Barbara exits

Olive It's nice that Mrs Lane has been able to dance. She has
  looked a bit lonely all by herself. I wonder why SHE came here.

Jean Probably just because she liked the look of it, the same as we
  did. An island retreat, away from it all.

Olive But it's an odd place to come to all by yourself, don't you
  think?

Jean On the contrary. I think it's ideal.

Olive In what way?

Jean Because it is such a tiny island with nothing on it except the
  hotel. It's like a small community, and everyone on the island is
  a part of it. It's much better than being in a big place like
  Torquay or Bournemouth say, where you walk out of your hotel
  and everyone is a stranger. Here everyone knows everyone, at
  least by sight, within a few hours of their arrival.

Olive That's true. I hadn't thought of it like that. You are quite
  right of course, but then you always are ... always were.

Jean Someone in the family had to get the brains. You certainly
  got all the beauty.

Olive Much good it did me.

Jean Oh, I don't know. You did all right.

Olive A divorcee! If you can call that all right!

Jean But look at the settlement you got.

Olive And the nervous breakdown to go with it.

Jean Don't exaggerate.

Olive I was very upset. I loved Ronald ... Well, I was fond of him.

Jean But not fond enough to put up with his shenanigans.

Olive Certainly not!

Jean Never mind, it's all over now. Put it all behind you and enjoy
  your holiday.

Olive Yes, I must. Thanks for being such a brick.

Jean Well, what are sisters for?

The music starts again

Have you had enough tea? Shall we go through to the ballroom again?

Olive Might as well.

Jean and Olive exit to the ballroom

Lucy, the maid, comes in to clear the tea things. Whilst she is doing so a Woman, wearing a long coat, headscarf and dark glasses, comes in, sees Lucy and stops

Lucy Good afternoon, madam. Would you like some tea?

The Woman shakes her head, puts her hand up to cover her mouth and hurries out

Lucy shrugs, picks up the tray and is about to leave when:

Barbara enters, looking over her shoulder as she does

Barbara I say, who was that?

Lucy I really don't know, madam. I believe the lady arrived last night and is leaving this afternoon.

Barbara Funny ... She looked just like ... not that you could really see her face ... no, it couldn't be.

Lucy Who, madam?

Barbara Take no notice, it's just my imagination. Off you go.

Lucy Yes, madam. (*She starts to leave*)

Barbara Oh, Lucy.

Lucy Yes, madam?

Barbara I suppose the lady would have signed the register when she came.

Lucy I really couldn't say, madam.

Lucy exits with the tea tray

After a moment or two Barbara shrugs and goes into the ballroom

Shortly afterwards the music stops and applause is heard

Mrs Chisholm, followed by her secretary Miss Mary Day, enter from the ballroom. They sit at a table

Mrs Chisholm I don't think we need to suffer any more of that nonsense. I've got all I need. Make a few notes, will you, Mary?

Mary gets out a notepad and makes notes as Mrs Chisholm dictates

Dances last approximately three and a half minutes. Intervals between dances vary from one minute to five . . .

Mary Depending on whether the band requires refreshment!

Mrs Chisholm Yes, that makes it a bit complicated. Anyway, to continue—usually one person or more leaves or enters the ballroom between each dance, but no one seems to leave while the dance is in progress. I think that's all for now. Ah, just one more thing, interesting point this, most of the dresses are pink. (*Or whatever colour is appropriate*)

Mary (*writing*) "Pink". Is that significant?

Mrs Chisholm It could be. One would be less likely to notice who had gone out or come in.

Mary Yes, of course, I see now. (*She shuts her notepad*) How does that fit in with your plot?

Mrs Chisholm (*confidentially*) Well now. We've got to get the poison somewhere where the woman takes it in full view of everyone else, but make sure no one else can take it by mistake. Now—if I wait until the end of a dance I can take Francesca out, wearing a pink frock of course, assuming that no one will come out while the band is playing. That will give her time to go to her room, slip out through the window and . . . um . . . I'm not quite sure about the next bit . . .

Jean enters at this point and overhears the last part of Mrs Chisholm's speech

(*She leans forward, confidentially*) . . . but one thing I am sure of—we can get the poison into that woman while the tea dance is on, in full view of everyone, and no one will ever be able to find out how it was done.

Jean is horrified at what she has heard and backs out of the room

Mrs Chisholm and Mary are unaware that Jean has overheard them

Olive (*off*) Get a move on, Jean, you're holding up the traffic

Olive enters, pushing Jean in front of her

(*To Mrs Chisholm*) Do you mind if we join you? It's a bit warm in the ballroom. (*She sits*) I suppose we are silly to be indoors at all on such a lovely afternoon, but I do so enjoy listening to the orchestra while I am having my tea. It is one of the most charming features of the hotel, don't you think? Anyway, we went for a long walk along the beach after lunch, didn't we, Jean? Jean, whatever is the matter with you? Do come and sit down.

Jean does so reluctantly and as far away as politely possible

In fact we went so far we nearly got cut off by the tide. Another few minutes and we would have had to take our shoes and stockings off and paddle home. By the way, I don't think we have been introduced. I am Olive Adams and this is my sister, Jean Barbour.

Mrs Chisholm (*introducing herself reluctantly*) Mrs Chisholm. My companion Miss Day.

Olive (*chattering on*) Have you just arrived? We haven't seen you before, have we, Jean? We've been here a week now. Isn't it a lovely hotel, so romantic being on an island. Have you been before or is this your first visit?

Mrs Chisholm Yes, it is a lovely hotel and yes, we only arrived today, but it is not my first visit by a long way. I stay here quite often. It suits my purpose admirably.

Olive And what would your purpose be, Mrs Chisholm?

Mrs Chisholm Ah, that would be telling.

Olive Goodness, how mysterious. We are quite intrigued, aren't we, Jean?

Jean Mm? Oh, yes, quite intrigued. Olive, don't you think it would be a good idea to go to our rooms and have a little rest— all that walking and dancing . . .

Olive Goodness no. What a waste of a delightful afternoon. No, I shall stay here and chat.

Mrs Chisholm (*standing up*) If you don't mind I think I shall go to my room. I need to do some quiet thinking. Come along, Mary.

Mrs Chisholm and Mary exit

Jean (*sitting beside Olive*) That woman . . .

Olive What do you mean, "that woman". She seems quite nice. Not very sociable maybe, but . . .

Jean You don't know what I know. She is not very nice at all. In fact she is plotting to murder someone.

Olive Don't be ridiculous. What absolute nonsense.

Jean It's true, I tell you. I heard her.

Olive Heard her plotting to murder someone! How?

Jean POISON!

Olive Oh Jean, don't be so ridiculous. Who is she going to poison?

Jean I don't know. She didn't say. Obviously she didn't say who, but it was definitely a woman. I did gather that much.

Olive Do you mean to tell me that . . .

Jean Sh. Someone's coming.

Barbara enters from ballroom

Barbara I've handed my gallant knight back to his lady wife and as there don't seem to be any more spare gentlemen Cinderella must leave the ball. Perhaps I'll go for a walk. What is the tide doing? (*She goes to the window*)

Jean I'm afraid it's high at the moment. You won't be able to walk yet.

Barbara (*looking out of the window*) So it is. I say! Have you seen that yacht out in the bay?

Olive (*going to look out of the window*) Wow! What a beauty!

Jean (*joining them*) That wasn't there earlier this afternoon. It must have just come in. I wonder who it belongs to.

Barbara Whoever it is, he must be jolly wealthy. (*She picks up the binoculars and looks out*) There's a launch alongside. Do you think they are coming ashore here? Now that would be just the thing for us, wouldn't it? Three rich young bachelors—or three wealthy old widowers if you prefer. One each. Bags me first pick.

Olive You can count me out. I'm rather off men at the moment, thank you.

Barbara Really! Why is that?

Jean My sister has just divorced her husband.

Barbara I'm sorry. I didn't know. That must be nearly as traumatic as being widowed.

Olive Oh, surely not. Except for the stigma. Being widowed is perfectly respectable, being divorced is not, even when one is the innocent party.

Jean (*still looking through the binoculars*) That launch does seem to be coming this way, but it only has one person in it. Looks like a crew member from his cap.

Barbara Dash! Another fantasy bites the dust. No handsome
prince to carry me off. Which reminds me—

Barbara moves to the centre of the room, followed by the others

—talking of princes—and divorcees—have you seen that mysterious woman who arrived yesterday?

Olive What woman?

Jean Why mysterious?

Barbara I bumped into her in the hall a little while ago. She had a
headscarf on and dark glasses, and she put her hand over her
face when she saw me. I asked Lucy, the maid, who it was, but
she didn't know anything about her, only that she had arrived
last night and was leaving this afternoon.

Jean So how does that make her so mysterious?

Barbara Well ... Oh, I expect it was just my imagination. As I
said, she did have dark glasses on and I only caught a glimpse of
her face, but ...

Jean But what?

Barbara Well, I could have sworn it was ... Wallis Simpson.

Olive (*shrieking*) WALLIS SIMPSON!

Barbara Sshh! It's obvious no-one is supposed to know she is
here.

Jean But are you sure it was her?

Barbara No, of course I'm not sure, but it did look awfully like
her and she was quite obviously really upset that I'd seen her.

Olive But what would Wallis Simpson be doing here, in this
remote corner of Devon.

Barbara But don't you think this is just the sort of place she would
come to, away from all the publicity. She'd be safe enough
here ...

Jean gasps, horrified

Olive Jean, whatever is the matter?

Jean (*in a strangled voice*) MURDER!

Olive (*shocked*) Oh no! (*Disbelievingly*) Oh no.

Barbara What murder? What are you talking about?

Jean (*whispering*) I overheard a conversation, a plot, to murder
some woman during the tea dance. They must have meant ...

Barbara (*horrified*) Mrs Simpson!

They are all struck dumb by the enormity of their discovery. The music swells and dies. Applause is heard. They all look at the doorway, but no one comes or goes and the music starts again

Jean We have got to do something.

Olive What can we do?

Jean I don't know. Let me think.

Barbara Who was planning this murder, or didn't you see?

Jean I saw all right. It was Mrs . . . What was her name?

Olive Mrs Chisholm, and that other woman she said was her companion, Miss Day.

Barbara I don't think I know them.

Olive They only arrived today. (*She describes Mrs Chisholm as appropriate*)

Barbara Oh yes, I know who you mean. They were having tea in the ballroom. But she can't be a murderer . . . murderess . . . she seemed quite pleasant. Kept herself to herself, didn't speak much to anyone except her companion. I really hardly noticed her.

Jean Exactly! She'd be bound to keep a low profile if she was planning a murder.

Olive But why would she want to murder Mrs Simpson?

Jean Political reasons. That's obvious. There are a lot of people in high places who would like to see Mrs Simpson out of the way. They are probably members of the secret service. I bet "Mrs Chisholm" isn't her real name.

Olive Oughtn't we to tell somebody? Ring the police?

Jean We can't do that, not if it's a secret service matter. They would never listen to us. No, we have got to do something ourselves.

Olive But what?

Barbara Sh! Someone's coming.

Lucy comes in with a tea tray and goes through into the ballroom

Olive Do you think we should tell HER?

Barbara Who? The maid?

Olive No, silly. Mrs Simpson.

Jean I don't suppose we would get a chance to speak to her. No, we must stop this "Mrs Chisholm" from getting to her.

Barbara How are we going to do that?

Jean First we must find out if Mrs Chisholm is still in her room.
Olive If she went to her room!

Lucy comes back from the ballroom

Jean Ah, Lucy, do you happen to know if Mrs Chisholm is in her room?
Lucy Mrs Chisholm? Oh, you mean . . . oh no . . . I don't think so, madam, she was sitting on the terrace a few minutes ago. Would you like me to take a message to her?
Jean No, thank you Lucy, it's not important.

Lucy goes to exit but pauses in the doorway

Lucy There's Mrs Chisholm and Miss Day coming now.

Mrs Chisholm and Mary enter

Have you finished on the terrace Mrs Chris . . . Mrs Chisholm? I'll bring the chairs in.
Mrs Chisholm Yes, thank you, Lucy. It's getting chilly now the sun has gone round.

Lucy exits

Mrs Chisholm and Mary come into the room, nod to the other ladies, and sit with their backs to them

Jean, Barbara and Olive mouth "what shall we do?", "I don't know" etc. to each other. The band strikes up a new tune

Barbara Oh, listen. They are playing (*name of tune*). That's my favourite. I must go and listen to it. Coming?
Jean Yes, all right. (*To Mrs Chisholm*) Excuse us.

Jean, Barbara and Olive leave, but Barbara comes back and stands just inside the room, listening

Mary Have you decided how you are going to dispose of the poison bottle?
Mrs Chisholm Toss it over the cliff I should think.
Mary But once the murder has been committed anyone leaving the hotel will be suspect.
Mrs Chisholm There won't be any hurry to dispose of it.
Mary But everyone will be searched, surely.

Mrs Chisholm But an innocent perfume bottle, carried in the handbag, and flaunted quite openly beforehand, like this. (*She opens her bag and takes out a bottle of cologne, holds it up, pretends to dab perfume behind her ears, then puts the bottle back*)

Barbara cannot control a gasp. Mrs Chisholm and Mary turn round. Barbara turns the gasp into a sneeze

Barbara Oh dear. Sorry. I was just going to my room to fetch a handkerchief.

Mary I do hope you haven't caught a chill.

Mrs Chisholm You wouldn't like anything so nasty to happen to you while you are on holiday, would you?

Barbara gives a little cry and runs off

Mrs Chisholm What was all that about?

Mary I can't imagine. She seemed quite upset.

Mrs Chisholm Very strange. Ah well, it's nothing to do with us. Now where was I?

Mary (*taking out her notepad*) Disposing of the perfume bottle.

Mrs Chisholm Ah yes. Make it eau de cologne, then it would seem quite natural to take it out and appear to dab some cologne on one's brow to calm oneself when the murder is discovered. The more obvious a thing is, the less likely it is to be noticed. A cologne bottle would be easier to fill anyway.

Mary Your usual meticulous attention to detail. It's no wonder you are such a success at your work.

Mrs Chisholm It is the details which are the most important. One silly mistake on my part, one false move, and half the civilized world would be howling for my blood as like as not.

Mary (*laughing*) Well, I don't think there is any fear of your making a mistake with this little intrigue. It is one of the most fiendish plots you have ever dreamed up. I am sure no one, no one at all, will guess who the murderer is.

Mrs Chisholm I hope not indeed. (*She gets up and goes to the window, picks up the binoculars and looks out*) Hm. Smart yacht out there. Wonder who that belongs to.

Mary joins Mrs Chisholm at the window

Barbara comes in stealthily, sees they are not looking her way and tiptoes across to the ballroom

Mrs Chisholm looks round and watches her, fascinated. Mary turns and looks, too

Curiouser and curiouser.

The both shrug and turn back to the window

Do you know anything about yachts, what sort that is?

Mary Not much I'm afraid. I think it's a sloop or something like that. Or is it a schooner?

Mrs Chisholm It's very nice, whatever it is. Oh look, there's a cormorant, just dived off that rock. There. He's up again. Here, have a look. (*She passes the binoculars to Mary*) Can you see him?

Mary No ... oh yes, there he is. I think it's a shag, not a cormorant.

Mrs Chisholm What's the difference?

Mary I think a cormorant has a white face and a shag is all black, or is it the other way around?

During this conversation Olive, Jean and Barbara creep in from the ballroom with a great deal of pantomime, pushing each other ahead etc.

Barbara indicates the handbag with the dreaded perfume bottle, lying on a chair or table. Eventually one of them steps back onto another's foot, who lets out a squeak. Mrs Chisholm and Mary turn and see them

Mrs Chisholm Back again ladies. Has the dancing finished?

Jean Er no. (*She indicates the music still going on*)

Mrs Chisholm Ah yes. (*Waving her hand in time with the music*) Such a pretty tune—or don't you think so? Presumably not, as you have left the ballroom. (*Intrigued by their unease*) Is everything all right, you seem a little—*distrait*?

Olive Yes, of course we are all right. Is there any reason why we should not be?

Mrs Chisholm None that I know of, only you do look a little flushed. Would you like some eau de cologne to cool your forehead? I have some in my bag (*She moves towards her bag*)

Olive shrieks. Jean grabs Mrs Chisholm's arm and Barbara snatches up the bag

Barbara Oh no, you don't. We know all about you—you MUR-
DERESS. (*She takes the bottle from the handbag and flings it out
of the window*) That's foiled your little plot!

Mrs Chisholm (*brushing Jean aside*) Do you mind taking your
hands off me and telling me what this ridiculous charade is all
about?

Mary (*picking up the bag and replacing the contents*) Are you all
right?

Mrs Chisholm Yes, I'm all right (*She moves towards the door*) I
think I shall go to my room.

Jean (*leaping in front of her*) Oh no, you don't. You don't move
from this room until the police get here.

Olive Have you sent for the police then? I thought you said we
shouldn't.

Jean I've changed my mind. I think it's time we did.

Olive Shall I go and telephone?

Mrs Chisholm Just a minute. There seems to be some sort of
misunderstanding here. What am I supposed to have done?

Jean Nothing yet. Fortunately we were in time to prevent a most
terrible crime.

Mary What crime?

Olive Murder!

Mary Murder?

Mrs Chisholm starts to laugh

Barbara It's no use trying to laugh it off. We overheard every
word of your wicked plot.

Mrs Chisholm (*still laughing*) Oh dear, did you really?

Jean Yes, we did.

Mrs Chisholm But don't you see, that is just what it was you
heard—a plot. The plot of my new novel.

There is silence

Jean Novel?

Mary Don't you know who this is?

The shake their heads

Mary This is Agatha Christie.

Olive THE Agatha Christie, who writes all those detective stories?

Mrs Chisholm The very same.

Olive Oh.

Barbara I'm sorry, but I just don't believe it. It is too much of a coincidence. I distinctly overheard Mrs Chisholm saying she was going to poison "The Woman" during the tea dance with poison in a perfume bottle.

Mrs Chisholm So that is why you threw my eau de cologne out of the window/But I told you, it is the plot for my next book.

Barbara And I suppose you are going to tell me that it is just a coincidence that a very particular woman is here in this hotel at this very moment—in disguise of course.

Mrs Chisholm What woman? I have no idea what you are talking about.

Barbara Oh yes, you have. You know exactly who I mean.

Mrs Chisholm Indeed I do not.

Mary What woman?

Barbara I saw her in the corridor, just a glimpse, but I knew who it was.

Mrs Chisholm Who was it?

Olive Mrs Simpson.

Mary Mrs Simpson!!

Jean
Barbara } (*together*) Sshh!
Olive

Barbara So you see, your story doesn't sound very convincing to us.

Mrs Chisholm This is ridiculous. Ah. Just a minute (*She goes to the bookcase*) I'm sure they have . . . yes, here we are. (*She selects a book and hands it to Jean*)

Jean (*studying the book, front and back*) Umhm. I'm afraid we *have* rather made fools of ourselves. Look. It *is* Agatha Christie. Here's one of her books with her picture on the dust jacket. (*She shows the book to the others*) I am most terribly sorry.

Barbara Oh, dear. Your perfume. You must let me get you some more. I'm so sorry.

Mrs Chisholm That's quite all right. Apologies accepted. What a fright I must have given you. Oh dear, oh dear. (*Laughing*) Mary, how do you fancy yourself as a murderess—or at least an accomplice?

Mary Particularly to the murder of Wallis Simpson.

Mrs Chisholm (*seriously*) Are you sure that's who it was?

Barbara Pretty sure. I wasn't at first. As I said, I only caught a glimpse of her and she hid her face like this (*She covers her mouth*) But she looked really annoyed at being seen. I checked in the hotel register to see what she had signed herself as, but it just said "Mrs Smith", in block capitals, and "London" as the address, so that really convinced me.

Mrs Chisholm How very intriguing I wonder what she is doing here? I think we should all play detectives and try to track her down and get a proper look at her. I wonder which room she is in?

Lucy comes in

Mrs Chisholm Ah Lucy, just the one we want to see.

Lucy Yes, madam?

Barbara Lucy, you know that lady I bumped into earlier this afternoon.

Lucy Yes madam, Mrs Smith.

Barbara Yes, that's right. Mrs Smith. Do you know if she is still here?

Lucy I think the poor lady has just left.

Mrs Chisholm "Poor lady"? Why, what is the matter with her?

Lucy Toothache, madam. Terrible toothache.

Mrs Chisholm Toothache?

Lucy Yes, madam. Apparently she was on her husband's yacht, sailing round the coast when she had this terrible toothache, so they put her ashore at Salcombe and she went to the dentist in Kingsbridge to have the tooth out, but she couldn't get back to the yacht last evening because of the tide, so she stayed the night here and her husband has just sent to fetch her. That's his yacht out there now. Will that be all, madam?

Mrs Chisholm Yes, thank you, Lucy.

Lucy exits

Barbara A lady with toothache!

Jean You and your Wallis Simpson!

Olive Oh, I am so disappointed. I was hoping to dine out on that story all next season.

Mrs Chisholm I think it is you who should be writing the mystery stories, not me. (*She looks at her watch*) Coming, Mary? The tea dance will be over at any moment and everyone will be wanting to get into the bathrooms before dinner. We shall get there first, while there is still plenty of hot water. Goodbye ladies. I have no doubt we shall meet again.

Olive Goodbye, Mrs "Chisholm". At least I shall be able to boast I met Agatha Christie, even if I didn't see Wallis Simpson.

Barbara Once again my apologies for throwing your perfume out of the window.

Mrs Chisholm Think nothing of it. It has been a most entertaining afternoon.

Mrs Chisholm and Mary exit

The others feel very flat after the excitement. Barbara picks up a magazine. Jean returns the book to the bookcase. Olive wanders to the window and picks up the binoculars to look out

Olive There's Mrs Smith going out to her husband's yacht. I do hope her toothache is better. Ah look, he's coming down the ladder to help her aboard. He is just . . . OH NO!

Barbara
Jean } *(together)* What is it?

Olive Well, I can't be absolutely sure, but he does look awfully like . . .

Jean *(grabbing the binoculars)* Let me see. My God! It can't be. It is!

Barbara *(grabbing the binoculars)* Let me see. *(Pause)* There! I told you so!

They all peer out of the window as

the CURTAIN *falls*

The tea dance is over. The band starts to play "God Save the King"

FURNITURE AND PROPERTY LIST

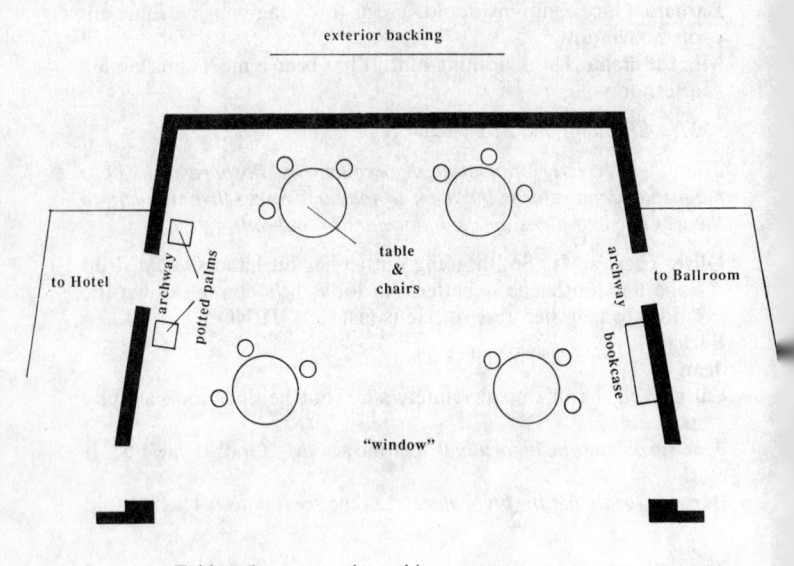

exterior backing

table & chairs

archway

potted palms

to Hotel

archway

bookcase

to Ballroom

"window"

On stage: Tables. *On one:* used tea things
Chairs
Potted palms
Binoculars
Carpet
Bookcase. *In it:* several books, including some by Agatha Christie. Magazines
Dressing as required

Off stage: Tea tray (**Lucy**)

Personal: **Olive:** handbag
Jean: handbag
Barbara: handbag, fan
Mary: handbag containing notepad and pencil
Mrs Chisholm: handbag containing cologne bottle, items of dressing

LIGHTING PLOT

One interior setting. Afternoon sunshine. No practical fittings required

No cues

EFFECTS PLOT

MADE AND PRINTED IN GREAT BRITAIN BY
LATIMER TREND & COMPANY LTD PLYMOUTH

MADE IN ENGLAND